# Decorating with
# Collectibles & Heirlooms

# Decorating with
# Collectibles & Heirlooms

## Connie Duran

Sterling Publishing Co., Inc.
New York

**Chapelle, Ltd.:**
  Jo Packham
  Sara Toliver
  Cindy Stoeckl

  Editor: Ray Cornia
  Editorial Director: Caroll Shreeve
  Art Director: Karla Haberstich
  Copy Editor: Marilyn Goff
  Graphic Illustrator: Kim Taylor
  Staff: Burgundy Alleman, Kelly Ashkettle, Areta Bingham,
    Emily Frandsen, Lana Hall, Susan Jorgensen, Barbara Milburn,
    Lecia Monsen, Karmen Quinney, Suzy Skadburg, Desirée Wybrow
  Photo Stylist: Connie Duran
  Photographer: Kevin Dilley

If you have any questions or comments, please contact:
Chapelle, Ltd., Inc., P.O. Box 9252, Ogden, UT 84409
  (801) 621-2777 • (801) 621-2788 Fax
  e-mail: chapelle@chapelleltd.com
  web site: www.chapelleltd.com

**Library of Congress Cataloging-in-Publication Data Available**

10 9 8 7 6 5 4 3 2 1

Published in paperback in 2005 by Sterling Publishing Co., Inc.
387 Park Avenue South, New York, NY 10016
Originally published under the title *Eclectic Style* by
Sterling Publishing Co., Inc.
© 2003 by Connie Duran
Distributed in Canada by Sterling Publishing
^c/o Canadian Manda Group, 165 Dufferin Street
Toronto, Ontario, Canada M6K 3H6
Distributed in Great Britain by Chrysalis Books Group PLC
The Chrysalis Building, Bramley Road, London W10 6SP, England
Distributed in Australia by Capricorn Link (Australia) Pty. Ltd.
P.O. Box 704, Windsor, NSW 2756, Australia
*Printed and Bound in China*
*All Rights Reserved*

Sterling ISBN  1-4027-0670-7  Hardcover
        ISBN  1-4027-2245-1  Paperback

# Preface

I like old things. I like to surround myself with objects that have an history and display some character. Naturally, such items do not always come in a set or in designer colors that automatically blend with the other elements of your home. Most vintage items need to be gently transformed into memorable treasures. Sometimes they must be carefully refinished or restored. Other times, the home must be refurbished to accommodate your favorite historical pieces. The right spot must be found or made for them.

In writing this book, I have attempted to show methods in various styles of decorating for how charming old objects can be used to bring beauty and character to your home. Throughout the book, I have given short descriptions on what was done to make items work together or give that special "look."

I encourage readers to combine their own personality with those treasured keepsakes that represent something to their family. The resulting arrangement will tell something about the home owners and the values they cherish.

*Annie Dawn*

# Contents

# Chapter 1

# Eclectic Chic

*I always love a fine "welcome home" to*
*well-loved things in a pleasing array.*

People who enjoy living with their heirlooms and collectibles usually want a lifestyle that is in harmony with the objects they cherish. The very nature of eclectic chic styling for interior design means putting together a look that supports both the way you live your active life and the way you feel about your personal space.

If you enjoy flowery porcelain dinnerware and service pieces because you inherited a set of exquisite Limoges china, then it may become a cornerstone of your styling. Not limited to the hutch or dining room, your flowery porcelain may appear in the bath, bedroom, entry, and so on. If you truly love it, then naturally you will want to see it as an art element in your home.

What comes into question is how you combine a particular item or collection of them harmoniously into your mixture of upholstered furniture, draperies, rugs, wallpaper, pictures, and so forth. That is where your personality and the tastes of those who share your household come into play. It may not be easy to merge the tastes and treasured objects from a variety of personalities into your home. However, not only can it be done—it can be a great deal of fun.

Whether you tackle nothing more daunting than the top of a nightstand or the mantel display in the living room, creating a small arrangement of special items is accomplished with the same principles of design that are used for a whole room or the entire house.

Paying attention to the sizes, shapes, colors, textures, and other such elements of art is as important as are the themes of the items and their meaning to family members. Varying heights, widths, contrasts, and odd numbers of items in arrangements apply at any scale.

*Right* Once embellished with gold, this antique picture frame was painted white, then lightly stained for a more romantic effect. The intricate detail in the wooden frame is much more evident now and can be picked up to repeat in throw pillows on the sofa below it.

The lamp, a $1.50 thrift-store purchase, had a few small chips around the base. I simply touched it up with a gold-leaf pen for a perfect match to this unusual shade.

Pillows have matching patterns in different hues, all echoing the texture of the frame's design elements above. All were found at a discount store on different shopping occasions.

My loft in a commercial building built in the late 1800s is located above my retail store, *Hen Feathers*. Original brick walls have been left exposed to make an historic style statement.

*Right* An antique floor lamp discovered at a thrift store for $15 stands stately beside an iron bench. This lamp has a story to tell—an history of its own—as does the bench and the room. I imagine there were stories read to children, a father reading the paper, a mother rocking her children to sleep, school studies accomplished under a warm glow. And by this same lamp's light, this book is written. Now I have become a part of its history as well.

Sometimes it is delightful to create an arrangement of items as though you are telling a story that a visitor—or yourself—might conjure up. Perhaps it is as if the props are still there, but the actors have just stepped off stage for a moment.

For example, at right, sitting delicately, rice paper roses with sprays of faux pearls tucked in and around add just a bit of romance. The story behind them might tell of a keepsake presented before or brought home after a cotillion dance or a wedding reception. The rose spray may have held a beribboned ring received at an engagement party. Who knows?

*My tastes run to a touch of history and romance captured in every room.*

*Left* I like to display things in an unexpected fashion, especially when I change a room around. Instead of hanging these pictures on the wall, I hung them on the back of the old iron bench. Their simple square shapes appear jewel-like and are a counterpoint to the softening effect of the decorative scroll shapes in the bench.

The gold-sprayed ornate leaf pattern of the frames makes them contrast dramatically to the flowing linework of the wrought-iron bench shapes. The bench has become even more romantic by adding sumptuous pillows stitched from leftover fabrics and embellished with loops of fringe.

# Tulle Frame Instructions

Favorite frame 4" x 4" (2)
Angel pictures from an old calendar
Piece of tulle (gold) 16 ½"–17" (cut in half)

Cut two pieces of tulle. Tuck tulle over and around edges of each picture. Using a butter knife, smooth tulle under glass. Secure picture, tulle, and glass in frame.

*Right* A small space between windows is a perfect spot for a collection of brass hooks or small pictures discovered at garage sales and thrift stores. The antique mirror and brass towel holder complement the arrangement. Note the wire spray of faux pearls wrapped around the towel bar. Intended as a Christmas decoration, I liked the way it softened the lines of the bar.

The shade on the antique floor lamp, another thrift-store purchase of $10, is stained and tattered; however, I simply could not part with it and the many years of wear it makes known. I particularly enjoy the way this wall arrangement repeats my favored shade in the mirror.

Using a mixed collection of items in a non-traditional approach is a chic way to enjoy their eclectic appeal. Not every arrangement has to have a functional use beyond creating a focal point of visual interest.

An important consideration in this wall treatment is the uniform presence of similarly muted colors in each framed print.

Begin with a simple wooden birdhouse. Nail or glue on halved wooden turnings and mitered frame material or molding scraps to finish.

16

*Above* This charming vignette is all about history and childhood whimsey. Atop an antique wooden chest, metal rabbit bookends serve to hold a private collection of vintage leather-bound books and a family Bible. Setting them off with an odd number of white silk rosebuds to complement the white couch brings the entire arrangement into a restful harmony that is no less than elegant. Combining the rustic childlike rabbits with the roses is an unexpected contradiction that is very chic.

Since the bookends are very dark in value, they must be arranged against white or a very light background in order to be properly appreciated for their form and delicate detail. When setting up similar vignettes in your home, consider the dark and light qualities of each object and how they contrast with one another.

*Opposite* A birdhouse made from salvaged pieces from an old hotel in Monterey, California, is placed in front of a tall window covered with sheer draperies. Letting the diffused light in adds an inviting romantic note to the room, while it obscures the view of the adjacent buildings and provides privacy.

The sheers also act as a subtle backdrop to this eclectic shabby-chic-style art piece. Though you may not have an opportunity to scavenge marvelous architectural fragments, it is possible to make a birdhouse with home-improvement-store scraps.

## Accessories

I prefer decorating my spaces with surprising touches which express my personality and tastes in my home.

Note how the eye is carried upward by the sheer curtains and sustained on the way down with three—again an odd number—of three-armed similar metal candelabrum at three different heights. In your mind's eye you can draw a stable triangle between them. Chunky furniture anchors the delicate accessories in the room.

## Style

When I enter the room featured at right, I feel surrounded by softness, stillness, and serenity in an embracing manner. I feel feminine, soothed, calmed, and comforted.

The soft carpet and the numerous sheer curtains used for a privacy divider and draperies add tranquility to this one-room apartment space. Furniture is arranged to further define living spaces in one big room. Keeping the color palette simple adds to the peacefulness.

## Texture

One of the most important design elements of all—texture—was employed in the styling decisions for this room.

The room would not feel as feminine and serene if the drapery fabric had been heavy and/or ornate with a busy pattern. All of the filmy sheer quality that allows diffused light to pass into every area of the space is a critical part of the success of this airy welcoming room.

## Drapery Instructions

These "no-sew" sheer draperies are a breeze to create. Begin with a curtain rod 12" above the window, or suspended from the ceiling if you want them to hang as a room divider.

Cut fabric 8" longer than the height of the rod-to-floor measurement, so draperies can puddle.

Fold top of fabric over 1"–2" and attach drapery rings or hangers (clip rings, themed floral shower rings, or hooks) at regular intervals to allow for the depth of drapery scallop desired.

Sheer draperies in this room serve a dual purpose as a filmy divider between sleeping area and living space as well as filtering light for a soft gentle mood.

*Above* A working Big Ben alarm clock found at a garage sale for $1 sits unpretentiously atop a bedside table beneath a picture of my grandmother. Sometimes the minimal use of single, aligned items in an arrangement such as this *is* the unexpected.

*Right* Enveloping the bed in more sheers for a canopy-style treatment increases the sense of romance, privacy, and comfort. The silk dupioni duvet and pillows in pearl and earthy metallic tones is a luxurious counterpoint to the rustic bedstead for an expression of unexpected style.

*Enjoy nature's grace in the curve of her branches.*

*Left* An inexpensive vase filled with twigs and large white flowers rests upon a bedside table. A piece of leftover fabric tucked in and around the vase conceals the transparent glass and its twig contents. Once again, something simple yet unexpected adds a touch of romance. Adding another framed picture and a sparkling candle wall sconce, placed and hung so it fits inside the branches, fills this space perfectly.

When creating small vignettes, start with large items and fill in the open spaces with small treasures. As here, the vase of branches and three prominent flower heads are visually appreciated as one large item.

In nature we find a harmony of form, rhythm, texture, and pattern already figured out for us to repeat in our interiors. The distressed white table and the neutral wall color set the color palette to follow: A white fabric scrap to cover the vase, white blossoms, white candles, white art in a clear frame, and simple dark branches and metal sconce arms are a design study in complementary rhythm.

*Opposite* A small wall in my bedroom is where I chose to display some favorite pictures of my mother and her mother. All but two of the photos are matted with authentic vintage mats I found at antique stores. I framed them with a variety of complementary molding styles that enhance their eclectic look.

*Right* When it comes to arranging quite dissimilar items in a variety of shapes, sizes, widths, and heights, we can always rely on simplicity and odd numbers.

Prominent in this corner of the room is an arrangement of three warm-toned blossoms adding drama to a somber corner. On the wall are five portraits—again an odd number—in a single frame centered above a single round clock. Visualize the perfect triangle from the clock's pendulum to the bottom corners of the frame.

With the sconce and small frame gone from the table, this grouping of flowers, portraits and clock in odd numbers—one, three, five—works!

23

*Above* To carry the eye upward and soften the merging of a flat wall and a brick one, a top-of-cabinet vignette is the styling answer. Three candles form the apex of a triangle that is timely with a clock's face and a pair of cherubs in white, like the cabinet.

*Left* Two shelves with three levels of odd-numbered objects make an interesting wall arrangement. Note how the centered white bust and the face's tiny features act as the hub of the design. The five wall-sconce vases with flowers balance the shelves, their vertical supports, and the three open baskets with the stained-glass panel as a crown.

*Right* This rescued Victorian mirror in its gracefully curving frame inspired a focal point. Hanging it on the wall above the shabby-chic-style bureau, since I had distressed them to match, created the central idea.

Pairing other matched items symmetrically on either side brought a formality to the casual setting that pleases with its unexpectedness.

To give the same stability to this arrangement that support arms from bureaus to mirrors of this period originally had, I used the metal sconce-style vases. Stuffed loosely with white flowers and tied with white ribbons, they bridge the spaces between the furniture elements and tie the colors together.

The sconce vases alone were too short to be substantial enough in linking the design, so I added a pair of pale vintage prints at the level where curving mirror supports would have screwed into the mirror's frame.

*Left* In the arrangements atop the cabinet on these facing pages, the idea of less is more sets my vignette decisions. Each piece warrants an appreciative examination.

When I have a furniture piece I love and a strong background, as this cabinet and the brick wall, it is a pleasure to decorate one way one day and differently to fit my mood another day, by borrowing from other areas.

In keeping with the aged wall and distressed cabinet, objects selected to decorate the furniture need to have a sense of loved wear also. The rescued stained-glass panel, vintage print, and metal candlestick are in "time" harmony to the cabinet and the wall.

It would be an unexpected touch to incorporate one item that is quite new or very elegant and in perfectly preserved condition to express chic contrast to these aged items. A terrific area rug beneath the cabinet doors would also enhance a new look.

*Right* Without the framed print of the little girl and her magnificent dog, the brick wall comes more into play showing through the clear panes of the stained-glass panel. The wall is no longer a backdrop to the arrangement, but an integral part of the color palette. Red orange and blue green being complementary colors on a standard 12-color wheel, the visual appeal is subtle yet very viable in this strong symmetrical arrangement centered precisely on the distressed chest.

Because the distressed wall of the room is part of the décor, a shabby-chic-style chest is more in keeping with the tone of the space than a highly polished or intricately carved formal piece of furniture would be.

Having the cabinet painted white or a light color is necessary against such a deep color as the rustic brick wall. A dark piece of furniture would have simply canceled the beautifully contrasting effect.

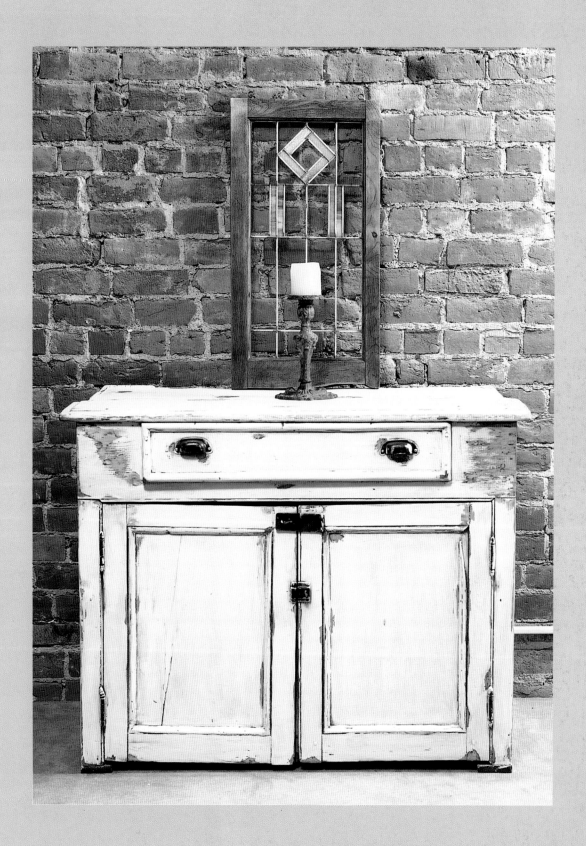

27

*Combine old and new in unexpected ways for styling surprise.*

*Right* An antique plate rack on the wall is symmetrically displayed with old books given to me as gifts and other cherished items instead of the expected plates. I filled empty spaces with framed pictures found at thrift and antique stores. I did nothing to repair or refinish any of them, as I love the look of aged things.

A simple arrangement of dried roses given by a loved one is centered on the shelf of the plate rack. Fresh roses are the central focus on the table. The three framed prints behind them on the wall become a background that stabilizes the wall arrangement.

A picture for which I have not found the perfect spot sits at the base of the table and obscures an electrical outlet. Could this be the right place for it?

The right side of the framed art beneath the metal table runs through the invisible center of the vase above it, thus anchoring all of the items from wall to floor.

*Left* An important part of the pleasure of decorating our homes with eclectic items gathered from a variety of sources is rearranging them whenever the mood or need arises.

The dark brick wall and the contrasting white-painted chest look quite different when the arch-paned window with matted photos is displayed here.

Because the wall is rich in color and dark in value, the dark frame merges with the wall and allows the photos themselves to stand out by contrast. Their lighter values are more akin to the chest, which I really love for its marvelous detail and distressing.

*Above* For an unexpected dining event, I framed vintage prints and used them as "place mats" at the setting for each guest. A white silk rose adds a delicate counterpoint accent to the rough texture of the table.

*Opposite* The farmhouse table and wonderful armoire for dishes and collectibles establish the vintage theme of this dining room. I brought the birdhouse from the living-room area to anchor the corner with a style statement in harmony with the furniture.

Since the table was constructed of salvaged wood from old torn-down homes, I complemented it with an eclectic variety of thrift-store and garage-sale chairs. They were painted and distressed to match one another.

*A beautifully appointed table makes every guest welcome.*

*Above* Related colors of white, ivory, cream, and pale butter yellow have been exploited to unify a variety of accessories brought from nature, the china cabinet, and the craft store.

*Right* A single paper rose with a note attached by a sheer shimmery ribbon and placed on a plate could say "I love you," "thank-you," or simply be a guest favor to keep.

*Opposite* Decorating a table for a festive occasion is an ideal time to combine favorite eclectic items within a theme. Artfully combining ceramic pots and angel busts, vases filled with three white roses and surrounded by tiny white flowers, large white candelabrum with white candles and white china make for an elegant style statement arranged on flowing white table linens.

*Below* For just a touch of color in an all-white hutch, I have placed dried red roses among the white paper ones. Note how I chose again the odd-number technique to style three matching pots; then for an asymmetrical arrangement, three textured pears around the base of one pot balanced by one white rose on the opposite side.

*Opposite* An antique mirror hung inside of a refinished hutch lends a touch of romance and an element of surprise. The mirror adds the sparkle of light and reflection to the low-light interior of the hutch.

# Fabric Mirror Instructions

Remove mirror from frame. Clean and paint frame with two coats white satin. Distress raised edges and corners of frame where natural wear may occur, using medium-grit sandpaper. Stain lightly with oak-colored stain, immediately rubbing off excess with a soft cloth. Reapply stain to areas you want darker. Wipe again. Lay mirror on desired fabric. Foam-core board, available at any frame shop, may be substituted for mirror. Cut an additional 2" around all sides of mirror. Use double-sided tape to attach fabric to mirror. Secure covered mirror into frame and hang.

*Right* A vintage appearance to this wire reproduction antique shelf was achieved by painting, then sanding, staining, and wiping until an aged quality pleased me. Feeling the need for balance on the wall above, I centered and mounted a print of a little girl in a distressed frame, allowing just enough room for a row of potted flowers.

I liked the contrast of the pale colored pots and white paper roses, as well as the white dishes against the rich tone of the wall.

I used a matched pair of plates on the middle shelf, rather than using the odd-number principle of design alone. The framed picture, the three pots, and the two plates total six elements. From these elements, a balanced triangular shape has been created. Using the pair of plates and the three pots makes the odd-number principle work.

Remember that one is an odd number and a single item can often hold its own in a design. Leaving the bottom shelf empty allows the metalwork diamond and scroll patterns to shine.

*Left* What turned out to be a stunning old secretary is a recycled piece of furniture that I found on a curbside awaiting the waste-disposal truck. It was broken and gray with water damage. I had it professionally repaired, then I stained and varnished it. Thus transformed, it is the beautiful piece you see here.

*Right* The print of the little girl and her Great Dane looks differently here than when placed on the white cabinet with the stained-glass panel on page 26. It fits nicely into the scale of this new arrangement.

The same secretary as above has an entirely different styling feel when an antique chair is placed in front of it, with a vignette arrangement on its velvet seat. The framed print leans on the chair back. The metal candlestick and three old volumes complete the triangle.

On the floor, a metal container holds a splash of white silk roses to anchor the candle's color. The white rabbits and aged clock face form another triangle with the candle and roses. The deceptively simple design has classic components.

*Below* It was logical to theme this arrangement around the historical period of the charming mantel clock, the secretary, and the brick wall of the building itself. The oriental ivory carving of rabbits is older yet fits the look.

The mantel clock is a reproduction piece. By distressing it with a bit of sandpaper to roughen the likely areas for natural wear over time, it appears authentically vintage.

*Left* This smiling frog figurine brings a touch of whimsy to an end table in my living room. He is the epitome of the delightfully unexpected in decorating accessories. The bowl he holds can be filled with faux items, snacks, soaps, gloves and keys, etc., according to where I place him.

*Opposite* A bathroom cupboard is transformed by arranging four of the same prints on its shelves. Whimsy is introduced in surprising scale, with a pair of white miniature iron rockers. Antique lace draped at the top is complemented with roses and the vintage floral print and glass holder on the wall. Shelves could hold stacks of rolled hand towels or decorative bottles filled with shampoo, bubble bath, and cotton balls.

# Chapter 2

# Eclectic Farmhouse

*Gracious country living takes me home again to times with my grandmother.*

What is almost as marvelous an experience as decorating one's own home is being invited to style someone else's. When I can add to that the joy of nostalgia recalling a slower-paced lifestyle, family gatherings that flow indoors and outside, and expanses of lush countryside and nature's bounty, it is bound to be country.

If there is one luxury to a farmhouse that city dwellers pine for, it is space. Houses in the country are "approached" by fence-lined lanes, pathways, porches, or spacious verandas. Views may take the eye to the horizon, or in the least to the abundance of a garden. One does not simply step from curb to front door.

Rooms have more than adequate space for family activities and allow for extended family members, friends, and indoor and outdoor pets. Farmhouses, be they antique or reproduction, may be constructed all on one floor, or on two or more levels. There may be dormers, side porches, pillars, fireplaces, and plenty of windows.

Styling a farmhouse gave me a big canvas, so to speak, on which to "paint" a livable and comfortable gracious country ambience for an active young family.

Beginning with the "feel" of a farmhouse—a grandmother's house—a white picket fence with roosters at the gate and hanging flowers establish the style.

The design techniques employed in any styling challenge are present here, but on a grander scale in terms of space. However, the grander scale is balanced by the concept of a simpler, more casual and spontaneous lifestyle. The attention to detail of country living will include displaying eclectic, lovingly worn, and handmade items handed down or appearing to have been so.

*Right* Before one even enters this farmhouse, the picket fence returns us to the charm of an earlier simple and gracious time.

Our eye is led to the fence and home by a path made from recycled cement salvaged from a torn-out driveway. To soften the approach and enhance its welcome to visitors, aromatic herbs are planted in the spaces between the pieces of broken concrete. Pleasing aromas are released as visitors step on them while walking to the front door.

Decorative shutters recall a time when shutters were an essential protection to precious glass panes that had to be imported.

The arbor gate, hanging baskets, and abundant flowers help us remember a time when women beautified their yards with flowers and brought fresh vegetables and herbs from the garden. The family gathered after supper on such a porch to rest after a day of chores.

*Left* The white picket fence on each side of the farmhouse driveway is a perfect backdrop for brightly colored flower beds. The gate is the perfect backdrop for a French country metal flower basket—the surprising container for metal angels. They both greet visitors and keep watch over the family.

Each season or event can provide the opportunity for new styling ideas for an entry gate or fence post.

I enjoy encouraging home owners to style the porch railings and newel posts with floral or accent accessories that coordinate with the greeting arrangements on their gates. That way, as a visitor makes the journey from the road, along the path, and all the way to the gate and beyond, there is a pleasing natural progression.

Taking the flower and accessory theme another step further, it is easy to plan hanging baskets and potted plants in the same color or flower plan.

*Left* A bright yellow forsythia wreath is a pleasant surprise hanging from the fence post. The contrast of the bright yellow and the burst of red dahlia blossoms against the white fence is typical of what we expect to see in the country. Such details clearly express the nostalgic essence of rural life: clean, fresh, beautiful, and fragrant.

For special occasions, a casually styled floral wreath can be spontaneously twisted from living branches, but the blossoms wilt quickly. However, since forsythia is one of the earliest to bloom of plants and dahlias come along much later in the summer, you can quickly see how a silk wreath of spring flowers can blend with growing natural plants in a seamless effect that only occasionally requires replenishing to keep a "just picked" appearance.

Placing them "behind" naturally blooming flowers makes them appear real. Silk flowers fade in strong natural light, so replace them often for a brilliant natural-looking wreath.

*Opposite* Looking at a comfortable, upholstered old empire-style chair in a grouping of other period items brings back memories of grandmother's or great-grandmother's house when I was a child.

Assembling keepsakes from storage and other rooms, plus some thrifty shopping stints, made this room's reading corner come together. A stack of old volumes for a lamp pedestal, a china dog for the mantel, and elaborate frames and complementing floral designs in the picture and the pillow recall the cozy country past. Lace, dyed draperies, and windows shaded with slatted blinds complete the look.

Centered on the wall beneath the framed art is an unexpected surprise. An empty foam frame embellished with faux cranberries hangs by metallic ribbon from a brass hook, appearing like a pendulum to the frame above.

*Right* Larger-than-life wallpaper flowers transport us to a farmhouse garden. Dramatic wallcoverings steal the limelight, so it was best to understate the furniture and decorative elements. The garage-sale table cost $1 and staining effort. Blossoms invited bunnies to join the handsome boy, completing an imagined story.

*Right* A dresser found in perfect shape was such a delight that not improving upon the cabinet-maker's elegant design seemed to be the superb styling idea.

I adorned it simply to not detract from the beauty of its carvings and robust vintage knobs. Books are centered and stacked atop the piece. A charming framed animal print hung directly above required nothing more than a pair of perched sparrows—much to the imagined amusement of the fluffy pair of kittens within pouncing view. It is such fun to make up stories when arranging simple eclectic items.

Imagine how unconnected the print and the birds would appear without a stack of books for height. An alternative book and bird vignette above is held in the circle of a doily.

*I enjoy arranging eclectic items to tell a story.*

*Left* As you look at this rocker are you reminded of a grandmother reading or perhaps mending her children's clothes as she ever so gently rocked? She may even have pieced together a quilt that she handed down to her children and grandchildren.

Just for decoration, the stack of books on the chair atop a lace dresser scarf can represent favorite skills and pastimes of those whom we remember with such affection.

Aligning the framed puppy print, the kitten print, and the antique rocker with its symbolic contents is a strong styling statement. The odd number of items makes one visual presence. It is also an example of how lovely one idea can be, as though a moment in time stood still while holding all of these memories in such a concentrated space.

Simplifying an arrangement of eclectic items makes a powerful message. And with so few items to move to actually use the chair, the styling feels less contrived. It is important for country to look practical.

*Above Left* A collection of floral-bouquet prints prompted a search for an array of vintage frames of uniform size and frame width. The result, after making the frames match in dark rich colors, is this pleasing arrangement of four pictures acting as one visual statement.

Note that though the flower prints are different from one another, each is a bouquet of similar size and has red and green in common to the others. I made certain to not select a print of a bouquet that would have called attention to itself and been disproportionate with the others.

*Above Right* A yard-sale discovery, this limed-oak veneer drop-leaf table was the height of fashion in the 1950s. Veneer does not hold up well, so restoration required a light sanding and a light coat of paint sloppily applied to show brush strokes. Once dry, it was lightly sanded on the natural-wear areas. A mason jar of flowers made a lovely vintage accent that echoes the floral-bouquet prints on the wall.

*Above* The simple beauty of these individual pieces of antique furniture is ideal for setting up a perfectly symmetrical arrangement. The center focal-point "anchoring" piece is the table with the white porcelain knob of its drawer acting as the hub of the arrangement. The white lamp base set precisely above it on the table's center establishes the apex of the design triangle. Its red and white shade forecasts the remaining opposing pair of corners of the triangle arrangement when the pair of matched chairs with their red seats are set at each side. Re-cover garage-sale chair seats by unscrewing them from the bottom. Lay the right side of seat down on the wrong side of fabric. Trace and cut with an extra 2"–3" on all sides. Add new stuffing, if necessary, before stapling fabric onto the seat with a staple gun.

*Colorful country styling is a challenge I love.*

*Opposite* Controlling intense color in eclectic items from different periods and styles is perhaps the greatest challenge of interior design. The size, shape, and placement of each element takes on extra importance in the overall plan. Open spaces; large bright prints; and dark, light, and neutral colors must all be kept in balance so as to not overwhelm the sense of cozy comfort in a country room.

Farm window views are part of this room's décor. Valances were made double the width of each window and hemmed with casings to slip over spring-loaded rods.

Symmetrical styling includes two pictures between the windows, centering the reupholstered couch in front. The flanking lamps were primed and painted white, then distressed and antiqued.

*Right* The rustic pig, a farm icon, echoes the lamp style of distressed white. Green frame and enamel-lined lidded English bread box accent with more green.

# Color

Red and white, used in checks on the lamp shade and ottoman and in floral prints for the chair and accents, are balanced by a sizable amount of soft green for the background in the upholstery fabric. It is picked up in the vase in the framed print and on the rim of the china plate behind this chair.

A red pillow over a white one accents both checkered and floral patterns, and creates a pleasing contrast to rest the eye against all of the busy floral patterns.

# Style

Country to me is cozy and comfortable as well as nostalgic. Creating the look required finding vintage items and refreshing them with fabric and paint so they worked together in harmony.

The floral-print upholstery fabric is echoed by the framed print, plate, and framed floral print on the floor behind the lamp—an unexpected placement that draws the eye to the chair.

The country-style counterpoint to all of the florals is gingham-checked fabric.

# Texture

Because textures can be visual or tactile, the most successful styling incorporates both. Pattern is considered a visual texture, as in the florals and checks. The actual tactile "feel" of fabric types, smooth porcelain and wood surfaces, and fringe on the pillows gives variety.

A comfortable balance with the abundance of textural variety in this room is achieved by maintaining restraint in the wall and floor treatments. Busy wallpaper or floral-patterned pillows would be overdone and uncomfortable.

# Accessories

The ottoman and chair were found at garage sales and reupholstered. Pillows were made to match the chair. The framed floral print above the chair was a flea-market find. The floor lamp was primed and painted white, then antiqued.

By combining the bold checks with bold florals, something our grandmothers would not have done with these fabrics, the unexpected in eclectic styling becomes a very chic statement. A small-checked red pillow is a subtler touch than matching the ottoman's checks.

*Above Left* Examples of how to not over-do with too many unbroken textural and pattern details are: layer a white pillow between floral ones; use a white lamp shade and white lace doily to settle a floral and beaded lamp.

*Below Left* The principle of successful contrast is easy to see in a colorful floral pillow against a white chair. In this case, having the chair upholstered with bedspread material gives that unexpected touch that makes the piece of furniture unique and memorable. The contrast created by the chair is combined with the other textural elements in the room to make a pleasing combination of color and tactile experiences.

*Opposite* Vintage and Victorian country items are married well in this nostalgic bedroom. Textures from chenille and lace to fringe, beads, and hand-stitched accents abound. Employ a white coverlet to balance a sea of double-ruffled floral pillows and dust ruffle. The black pillow, the black bedstead, and the painted hamper placed on the floor in front of the scrolled footboard are the perfect counterpoints to all of the white and florals.

*Left* The popularity of aqua has come and gone several times in decades of decorating. Whatever the wall color in a room I am decorating, I make certain that I use that color to my advantage.

Uniformly sized and painted white frames with textured patterns work beautifully when organized in grid arrangements. They contrast, or stand out, against expanses of strong color.

*Opposite* I arranged four framed prints with the largest as the center, then centered them to the dip in the shape of the chair back. By painting the frames and the metal chair to match, they counterbalance the floral print, scroll-patterned metal parts, and the strong colors of all the other elements. A simple white battenburg pillow finishes off the guest-room arrangement.

## Pad Cover Instructions

Vintage fabric, an old lace-edged drapery panel, or a tablecloth are ideal materials for making pillow covers. Measure and cut pieces for an "envelope" style pillowcase, then slip over a pillow.

Spray-paint a vintage or reproduction porch seat, roughen it lightly with sandpaper, rub on and then wipe off antiquing stain of your choice, then seal with polyurethane. Add a covered pad and your vintage pillow for chic style.

*Opposite* Who says country farmhouse style can't be fun? This beadboard wall treatment is quite up-to-the-moment with an unusual coat of pinkish lilac. The black tole tray collection is simply magic against that lively pink.

The clawfoot tub was found at a yard sale and professionally refinished. It is the perfect appointment to a country bath area, accented with a patterned rug.

*Right* The personality of this bathroom is enhanced by hanging a black tole tray on the door. A row of smaller trays positioned over the door continues the tole motif in harmony with the large and elaborately painted tray above the light switches. Without these decorations, the stripes on the wall would become overpowering.

*Above Right* Decorations on the bath chair can be changed to keep the design elements in the bathroom fresh and exciting.

*Opposite* Three rabbit figures in various poses, the wire basket of greens, and the straw hat and bear on the floral chair cushion are romantic woodsy details that make taking a bath a treat. A bath area large enough to include a dressing chair is luxury indeed. The wide tub surround allows for a pleasing mixture of practical and pretty items.

## Striped Wall Instructions

Begin by painting the entire room white. Two thorough coats should avoid any bleed through of undersurface blemishes. Decide the width of the seafoam-green stripes, taking into account doors, windows, and fixtures. Plumb, mark, tape off, and roller-paint green stripes per paint instructions.

*Above* There is nothing more farmhouse style than a porch with a wooden swing and a rocker. Complete the comfort and the look with vintage or reproduction country furniture for children and grown ups and a sprinkling of rural accessories.

From the brightly painted floor and rag rug, to the crockery, birdhouse, home-sewn quilt and vintage tablecloth, to the pillows and hanging house-number sign, each item adds authenticity to the scene. Color plays the dramatic role of bringing the country theme up-to-date. Red violet for the swing complements the blue violet floor and the yellow accents for a perfect 12-color wheel triad scheme. Note how the magenta stripes in the rug echo and ground the color of the swing.

*Above* This country look is a little more "homespun" and down-to-earth than the porch on the opposite page. Nothing bright and flashy here, just weathered wood flooring, a glow to a rubbed-oil finish on the glider bench, and chunky terra-cotta pots big enough to hold shrubs and young ornamental trees that can be transplanted to the yard later.

The porch style reflects the spaciousness of rural homes of the past, yet incorporates the convenience and beauty of container gardening. Oversized pillows and a well-stuffed glider cushion invite a relaxing afternoon with a good book or even a siesta. The floor is kept free of rugs and runners that up the maintenance factor. In windy areas, rugs may roll up or even blow away.

$\mathcal{A}bove$ I love to create the sort of unexpected surprise in a garden that is such a pleasure to make happen indoors. Here the items selected are a pair of garden boots, a watering can, a plastered brick wall, and some greenery. These items have been painted on a blank foundation wall. The wall was sealed with a waterproof acrylic finish.

The color tones of the mural are all related and have been carefully selected to enhance the natural flowers as they come into blooming season. The flowers planted in front of the mini mural add to the illusion and provide depth to the painting. They were purposely chosen for their small blossom heads, so that they would not overgrow the scale of the painting or totally cover it up. The bluish green of the live foliage is a wonderful complement to the rusty red faux brick and the green boots.

*Left* The country gazebo with gingerbread-trim embellishments has an appearance inspired by the theme of a genteel country home. Its uses and possibilities for decoration are limitless; but since it resides in the garden, it is a given that part of the decorations should include foliage and flowers. Accessories such as planters and outdoor furniture should be light enough to move easily so the gazebo can be rearranged for various activities and events.

*Right* One of the big advantages of potted flowers is that they can be introduced into areas such as a gazebo at the height of their bloom. Once the flowers have passed their prime, they can be replaced with blooms from a different season.

The ornate nature of the gazebo railings complements the wild profusion of flowers in the matching planter. Hanging baskets, planters, flowerpots, and urns should be used to place flowers in all locations and at all levels.

*Above* The pair of lambs grouped to one side of this old iron bench and out of the way of stepping are country-themed objects in appropriate scale to the bench.

*Opposite* An inexpensive bench has been primed, painted, and distressed, then waterproofed. Sitting among a flower bed just off the front porch, it makes a wonderful place to read, daydream, or gather one's thoughts.

*Above* An iron table sits in the garden year-round to weather naturally. A pair of cast-iron pots of differing heights have been planted with wheat grass, bringing the growing garden right to the table. A vintage watering can stands ready to be used, composing the third item in an arrangement so casual that it appears to have happened without plan. Such a table is ideal for garden parties to hold a tray of cold drinks and an ice bucket, or to use as an on-site potting spot. With the addition of a couple of chairs, it becomes an inviting seating area. Plus, it is lightweight enough to move.

*Left* An old waterproof watering can was transformed to a whimsical decorative element by first priming, then spray-painting it black. The black-and-white checkerboard rim pattern was stenciled on with acrylic paint, while the rest of the can was painted freehand. The white squares and polka dots echo the trellis.

The small aging iron trellis has been allowed to weather and rust. Against green foliage, the contrasting white curves of its scrolls blend well with the white blossoms of the natural plants that it supports.

*Above* A stone bench on a patio or near the garden path is a romantic enhancement to any country home. A whimsical addition is a barely visible stone frog hidden among the foliage—much as a real frog might be. A fanciful metal dragonfly on a wire spike adds to the fun and the charm.

*Above* An inexpensive potting bench was painted, distressed, and waterproofed. Decorative bird knobs were added in a contrasting color. Gardening tools sometimes give way to barbecue and tea party utensils. The dry-sink lid comes off to hold ice and canned beverages or bottled water.

*Opposite* Teas and barbecues, even breakfast or brunch, in a garden setting are so romantic. It is doubtful that such entertaining could occur very often with working farm folk of the past. However, most of us enjoy the nostalgia of old films and the landed gentry who had the means and the servants to make such events more commonplace.

With a backdrop of blue-violet lobelia in full bloom, how could afternoon garden tea not be memorable?

An old iron table and matching chairs have been painted with rustproof flat-black paint. The dark color makes the table and chairs seem more at home and timeless among the foliage. It takes little more to create the moment: an elegant china tea service, silver flatware, and vintage lace napkins and doily.

*Right* Served is a pound cake made from a favorite recipe baked in individual-sized bundt cake pans. It is garnished with a dollup of whipped cream, fresh berry fruits, and a freshly picked sprig of mint. What makes this dessert special is its country styling. A simple bundt cake is show-stopping country chic when presented on a gold-rimmed porcelain plate.

*I always enjoy styling for easy and appealing outdoor entertaining.*

# Chapter 3

# Eclectic Cottage

*Compact cottage spaces call for my
most creative design solutions.*

Cottage homes contain on average five or six rooms. In many areas of the country, they have no attics or basements for additional storage, bedroom, laundry, or play spaces. Living room, kitchen, a couple of bedrooms, and a bath are basic. Some cottages have a dining room or a breakfast nook as well, and occasionally a master bath off one of the bedrooms.

The rooms are not as spacious as farmhouse rooms. Furniture of any massive size may not even fit through the doors, let alone function well in such compact areas.

Designing cottage interiors is akin to arranging dollhouse furniture and accessories. Scale—meaning the relationship of sizes and spaces to one another—as well as function and comfort are critical considerations for planning a cottage-style home. Large homes can be arranged in terms of yards and feet, cottages by inches.

For a designer, cottages bring out one's ingenuity to make function and ease come together without sacrificing beauty and personality. Eclectic styling is my answer to all of these design challenges.

I begin with the owners' tastes, however different they may be in a multiperson family. Mixing and matching items that each individual enjoys collecting with colors they like, fabrics and patterns that please, and furniture in scale to the home come into my plan.

The decorating techniques for creating a home that supports a variety of lifestyle needs are the same for large homes as for small ones. The difference comes in the emphasis directed at the considerations of traffic patterns, how best to work and live in the spaces efficiently without a lot of clutter, and how to style for comfort and beauty. Keeping it simple works best.

*Right* Cottage-style decorating calls for many strategies to make space function easily in small areas with tight traffic patterns.

The amount of room between furniture pieces is "just enough" for drawers and doors to open and for people of modest proportions to move from place to place.

Contrary to what might seem logical, generous sizes in furniture should not be avoided just because space is at a premium. Note the chests and wing chairs in this room. Sitting areas will not feel inviting if furniture does not look sturdy enough to support people.

Balance is extra important to "settle" confined areas. For example, the frame of the center teapot print on the wall has no blue corners compared to those hung on either side. Three prints balance pleasantly four plates for a total of seven odd-numbered wall items. The white background chairs flank the brown table for stability of design with the wall art. The rectangular white box bridges the two.

# Color

To me, the feel of "cottage" is cheery and colorful. Bright yellows and blues sparkle as accents in checks and florals. Nature's color tones are my favorites for walls and floors to balance the intense brights with neutrals and muted colors.

Warm yellow walls in a soft pastel tint are a cheerful background for the pair of splashy floral-print chairs and many eclectic items. The various shapes, sizes, and prints are held in harmony with the repeated colors of yellow, blue, and white accented with red, green, and lilac.

# Style

Though this cottage's location could be city or coastal, the theme is sophisticated rustic country employing a happy mix of shabby-chic-style items, antiques, and some new reproductions.

A vignette example is the three objects in front of the rustic shutter. A white porcelain rooster and a white, with blue accent, candlestick and its bright yellow candle are arranged with a classic blue-and-white oriental ginger jar lamp. Topped by a simple white shade, the lamp and rooster balance the other lamp-and-rooster idea.

# Texture

This cottage room may be small, but it handles a wealth of textural diversity. Visual print patterns of florals and checks in upholstery and quilt shapes, striped upholstery, patterned teapot prints, and busy lamp-base designs are all relieved by great expanses of solid color and plain surface. A balance of busy to plain and simple is always important in cottage style.

Surface-texture variety is achieved through combining an antique tin ceiling tile, a weathered shutter, various fabrics, metal, and wood.

# Accessories

This cottage expresses the owners' eclectic and adventurous tastes. Old tin ceiling tile purchased at an antique store has been left outside to weather and rust, before mounting on the wall. The vintage shutter was purchased in Kansas City and simply set behind the chair.

The coffee table was distressed and sealed for a finish. It is decorated with the charm of a rustic birdhouse. Rag rugs, roosters, and quilts add to the expression of cottage style in this comfortable country theme.

This cottage room acts as dining room, conversation area, and game room according to what is on the table. The table itself can be turned to include those seated on the deacon's bench or in the rocker. Versatility in furniture use is basic to compact cottage styling.

*Above Left* Yellow, blue, and white florals, accentuated with red, and rooster motifs are sensational arranged with this antique high-backed deacon's bench. It was rescued from a rural pool hall owned by the home owner's grandfather. I squared up frames, bench, and floor tiles to stabilize active elements.

*Above Right* Wicker is perfect for cottage decorating because it is usually smaller and lighter in weight than upholstered furniture. It is flexible enough to add charm and practical function, wherever there is room to place it. Its appearance can be easily transformed, as was this garage-sale rocker, with spray paint. Whipping up a few bright pillows coordinates it into any room. Small-scale accents, such as the birdhouse and miniature captain's chair, give it more size presence by contrast.

*Opposite* A checkerboard-patterned floor was laid by starting in the middle of the floor and alternating tile colors, working out toward the wall, as per the manufacturer's instructions. Yellow and white chickens, the home owner's grandmother's handmade quilt as a table covering, and a wall pattern created from a grid on a white wall and painted in alternate squares of yellow give a fresh and unique look to this country cottage.

*Recycling architectural and thrift items is a way I enjoy making decorative accents.*

*Above* A vintage lace dresser scarf is lovely with a wooden tabletop peeking through. The table was constructed with wood from a demolition site. What child or grown-up would not enjoy coming home to fresh-baked oatmeal cookies and a mug of cold milk served on pretty pottery?

*Opposite* The door-frame-corner architectural piece was retrieved from a demolished Victorian home. The light fixture over the front door was found at a garage sale. Old wooden yarn spools have their own beauty. The bench table is a replica of one built in the 1800s. Carrying out the barnyard animal theme in prints and carved-wood figures adds to the overall rural cottage style.

*Above* Pegs for hanging things are necessary in a cottage home, but they need not receive ordinary style treatment. Here a wooden panel was distressed and painted with burnt-umber stain. A commercial fabricator and welder made the four metal bases to attach to the panel. Doorknobs found at antique stores were then fastened to the bases with screws. Whether the owners hang anything from them or not, the panel of knobs is a piece of art! Such an arrangement is also terrific for aprons in the kitchen, dog leashes by the back door, or art smocks in a painting area for children. In bedroom or bath, bathrobes, towels, and clothing could be kept similarly, stylishly at hand.

*Opposite* The standard wooden-knob panel that can be found assembled in unfinished-furniture stores can be made into a display board for framed art. Attach some organdy, chintz, or grosgrain ribbon to the backs of the frames and loop them over the knobs. Select ribbon or fabric colors that complement the other colors or patterns already going on in the room. Decide if the framed prints will be overpowered by the ribbon color and select accordingly.

*Left* In this more masculine cottage room, though the florals are not used, the rustic and eclectic collectibles are still prominent. Another weathered shutter plays backdrop for a vignette of boxes stacked in a graduated largest-to-smallest style, a toy horse, and primitive-style art.

The red cupboard was made by altering an old chest of drawers. The drawers were removed and doors were made from bead board, then trimmed with molding around the edges. The chest was painted with a satin finish, then distressed and lightly stained for a lovingly worn appearance, in keeping with the other items.

*Opposite* No roosters here! But angels float above the creatively upholstered empire sofa. Here florals are made more masculine with coordinating plaid, an old whitewashed farm stool, strong verticals in the birdhouse church spire, and the stack of round boxes. A wall shelf filled with miniatures is a centered focal point.

*Right* This star-studded themed interior is filled with a wide variety of references to the five-pointed star. Though this home owner took the idea in a patriotic direction, it need not be more than a star-themed approach.

Blue for stars in the wallpaper is a subtle backdrop to an eclectic mix of theme items with stars on fabric, metal, wood, and paint treatments.

Any favored color palette would work for such a room's design. Here the reds, whites, and blues are played out in strong colors as well as shades and tints. Note the pale blue of the old chest compared to the bright blue of the stars on the hanging cabinet and its rich dark blue top. Reds range from pastel to bright pink.

The playful accessories make this room ideal for a child. The sails on the toy boats did not originally have stars; they were stenciled on. The wooden star cutouts add sculptural effects.

Centering a red star between a pair of toy trucks atop the cabinet is another example of how the odd number of three can form a focal-point triangle. It is balanced in the reverse with the triangle of star-bordered fabric hanging in front of the drawers.

*Above* Another idea for decorating the red table is a framed quilt of stars for a focal point. Select three matching support items such as these star frames stuffed with patriotic-like ribbon for dimension and style.

*Left* Against a primarily white wall, the contrast of a red table makes it "sing" as the center of attention. The turned legs of the table are bead-like and repeated in the red beads draped around the star-embellished lamp.

Toy elements are carried out with the stuffed angel, the rocking horse, and the chunky white blocks with their carved yellow stars. A cut-out star on a simple red-stained shutter carries the star theme to the floor.

*Left* Wall shelf arrangements may be found, made, or purchased. Whether authentic vintage or some fresh creation, a shelved item such as this postman's box is a most unique and useful focal point in a cottage. It can simply be pretty for the sake of decoratively tying a room together, or it can tell a story about an individual's or an entire family's tastes, interests.

Painting the interior of each section white and the front edges and cornice green like the room made each segment into a tiny stage.

Empty space needs to be organized also. With six rows of four box shelves, a design pattern was worked out in triangles. Matched fabric-covered boxes in several sizes combine with three-dimensional objects to create a pleasing arrangement within the unit.

Echoed by the white sculpted base of the porcelain lamp and its simple white shade, the interior of the postman's box relates beautifully to the room's décor. The tiny items arranged on selective shelves take on the importance of a mini art gallery. Each family member could contribute an item that is meaningful to them to complete such an arrangement. Combine them with a good balance of color, size, and scale to the other items in the shelves and above them.

*Above* Though the furniture and accessories in this cottage bedroom are not precisely matched, the symmetrical arrangement is restful and serene. The placement of the mismatched side tables and lamps on either side of the centered bed gives stability to the variety of florals and accessories. Centering framed art above the headboard assists the calm design.

The bed's massive bead board, structural fence, and newel-post-style head- and footboards express solid support and stable design that is comforting for restful sleep.

For a bedroom to be restful, there can be a great deal of textural and accessory details going on, but color and pattern must be restrained. Soft pastels, a generous helping of white, and muted wall colors work best to promote a quiet atmosphere.

## Accessories

Architectural molding pieces, pretty boxes, and an array of fun frames can come together in a truly beautiful room with coordinated color.

For beds and sofas, benches and rockers, I enjoy layering giant pillows by size, pattern, ruffled edges, contrasting colors, and delicate pattern.

In bedrooms, I make certain to pull in decorative items that are white to keep the atmosphere restful. Eyes ready for sleep do not want to dart restlessly from color to brighter color.

## Style

Styling with photos, paintings, and prints in a collection of variously sized and decorative frames gives a room a personal statement.

Of course frames can be grouped on walls as previous pages have shown, but layering them in an overlapping design has more personality.

Organize the frames on a large surface, such as a mantel, a piano top, or as here on a chest at the foot of the bed. Place the largest at the back, then stagger rows down to the smallest.

## Texture

Texture that we can actually feel with our fingers is an important consideration in bedrooms, particularly for children and the elderly.

Chenille, lace, satin, flannel, brushed cotton, velvet, and linen fabrics come quickly to mind. Visual textures such as plump duvet-covered goose-down comforters and oversized pillows invite tumbling into bed for a good rest.

Ruffles and fringes, beads and ribbons are tactile and visual details I use in the bedroom.

## Frame Instructions

Gather a variety of thrift-shop frames, garage-sale finds, or create your own basic frame shapes in a variety of sizes.

Distress them with sandpaper, paint, or stain to suit your taste and the colors in the room.

Embellish each frame differently. Use painted or sticker details, such as polka dots, stripes, or hearts. Seal stickers with decoupage medium. Glue on decorative wooden cutouts and stamp or paint words and names around borders.

# Chapter 4

# Eclectic Nouveaux

*I combine eclectic elements simply,
to express the elegance of a new age.*

Every age has a few interior design styling trends that make it unique enough to say, that "looks like" the Victorian era or the '20s, '40s, '50s, and so on. Chinese and Japanese designs impacted many of those earlier decorative periods. Today, the influences of Oriental and Scandinavian simplicity are supported by the beauty and functional qualities of new materials.

Design styles such as those of the late Frank Lloyd Wright still inspire, as do structures of contemporary architects, landscape designers, and furniture makers.

Putting all of these influences together means we are designing interiors with fewer elements to distract from the whole. This fresh leaner, cleaner styling trend has given rise to a new decorating look for the twenty-first century. It allows for room to breathe new life into our living spaces as our lifestyles are changing.

People who enjoy collecting and displaying furniture from an eclectic variety of sources are more likely now than ever to do so with decorating restraint.

I support their desire to have a simple design approach that is not quite minimalist but leaning in that direction. The idea is to allow for a few strong elements to not be overwhelmed with too many decorative details. Eclectic nouveau to me means bringing the owners' favorite items and taste into the simplest combinations possible.

This look has a refreshing elegance that is recognizable for its economy of elements. It is distinctive and sophisticated and never fussy, even if items from fussier periods are displayed and used. The architectural structures of such homes are not disguised, but rather emphasized in this style. The "bones" of the home become part of the design, showing old brick, beams, and metal parts.

*The smallest of accent items*
*must key to your theme.*

*Above* On a mantelpiece or a shelf, a pair of carved or cast birds may add textural interest without being too "cute." Painted the same as the background they blend nicely. Enhance just one with a wreath, a ribbon, or a crown for an unexpected touch of whimsey and chic style.

*Opposite* Though the pair of framed art pieces with the vases of blooming branches for subject matter are not precisely the same, they are similar enough to appear to "match." Placed close together— much closer than one would ordinarily hang a pair of frames—their combined width is within the width of the sideboard cabinet. That design decision makes the entire arrangement work as one visual unit in the same way a headboard "completes" a bed.

By centering the urn of berries on the cabinet and nearly aligning it with the meeting point of the two frames, it becomes the subtle hub of the arrangement. Balancing the lamp and lidded box on either side supports the plan, but it is the textured vine and pairs of birds that actually link and balance the whole.

*Left* Earthbound styling was created to enhance the classical simplicity of the fireplace and its unique black box-shaped hearth. The architectural features of stepped-out dimensions from mantel to hearth box, and columns resting atop the unusually high hearth, are quite chic in this spare design.

Nature's theme is expressed in branches and twigs, warm earth colors, and three wild-bird statuary items.

The horizontal mirror doubles the images of the candleholders and emphasizes the wide fireplace. Dramatic reflective black fireplace tiles and raised hearth are repeated in dark vases.

## Fireplace Refinishing Instructions

This fireplace mantel was originally oak with a medium stain. A concrete patching compound was thickly applied and allowed to dry overnight. It was then sponge-painted using crumpled plastic wrap dipped in three separate colors of paint.

Rather than being made invisible, the stair railing was painted black to emphasize the importance of its form and color to the room.

## Color

The warm red wood of the cabinet sets the tone of the color palette. The frames on the wall and the brilliant rust-red rim of the torchère's flared glass are keyed in harmony. Within the upholstery weave on the chairs, there are flecks of that warm tone with neutrals for a pleasing balance.

The neutrals of taupe, cream, and black "settle" the red. Expanses of carpet, the buttery gold wall, and the foliage accents atop the cabinet serve to counter the intense red.

## Style

The pair of period club-style chairs are arranged to flank the elegantly carved cabinet. The highest point of each chair meets the top of the cabinet to complete a sweeping oval that embraces the ottoman at floor level—a stable and classic design plan.

The mirror is centered above the chairs and the decorative arrangement of items atop the cabinet create a steady right triangle. The mirror reflects the items styled in triangular order above the opposite cabinet to unite the room.

## Texture

This arrangement relies heavily on visual and tactile textures in balance and expressive contrast to one another.

The centered cabinet has a smooth surface and inviting touch. Nubby upholstery fabric on the chairs is in tactile contrast to the cabinet, while it is in harmony with the carpet and the velvety feel of the ottoman.

Tassels invite touch, as do the foliage accents on the cabinet and the plant by the right chair.

## Accessories

The pair of framed pictures on the right balances the torchère lamp with its large black tassel. White cord trim and tassel on the ottoman reverse the contrasting color accents.

Note how the space between the pair of pictures and the mirror is approximately equal to the width of the frames; and the curve of the ottoman's white cording completes the circle effect with the chairs. Even the peaked design on the cabinet doors emphasizes the sweep of the chair tops because of the chair placement.

*Left* The window's important swag treatment began with the decoration of its plaster curtain sconces. Each was painted flat black before bronze metallic highlights were rag-painted on.

Once dry and mounted on the window framework, the contrasting dark drapery fabric was threaded through and gracefully swagged.

The small antique table is centered and decorated with a dark classical stemmed vase stuffed casually with branches and flowers in the room's colors. Soft lighting from proportional table lamps and the chandelier complete the intimate setting.

The rich wood tones of the dining table, the antique table, and the chairs set the color palette, which contrasts with the metallic-colored walls and complements the fabric accents repeated in either softer or more-intense values.

# Painted Wall Instructions

The wall was sponge-painted with crumpled plastic wrap in three metallic colors: gold, copper, and bronze. The buffet was originally a liquor cabinet. The brass "candle" lamp is painted with "sophisticated" finishes of blackened bronze to create a metallic surface.

*Right* Mentioned before is the pleasure of designing a touch of surprise or romance into each room. In this focal point, both are distinctively present.

Bead trim was purchased and glued on around the edge of the lamp shade to add sparkle and to enhance the elaborate, romantic and surprisingly "empty" frame.

An urn of dried florals, placed behind and branching through the frame, gives dimension with style.

*Left* Plastic urns were painted a dark, unobtrusive tone that appears metallic or ceramic and more up-scale in sophistication than plastic. Each was then filled with green floral foam. Long twigs were arranged in the foam, three per urn, with dried moss used to cover the foam and act as a nature element. Small pear picks, matched in size and color, were inserted through the moss to secure them around the edge of each urn.

The paired-twig grouping and the lamp connect the framed art with the table. Note how the lamp shade was selected to repeat the vase in the painting, but upside down to its form—a subtle but important design touch. By matching the urns' color tone to the sculpted-bird candleholder, the rich wood elements— wide frame, "twiggy" chair, natural twigs, lamp, table—there is color unity within size and shape variety of design components.

*Right* Warm ivory and earth colors enhance the natural feel of this transition wall. Bridging work, seating, and traffic areas, the flow is an easy one with cues from the gently whorling twig wreath, the resting birds, and no embellishment to the armoire. The seven items atop the armoire exhibit a variety of graduating and balanced heights for interest.

Note how two of the birds, facing beak to beak, provide a very natural pause to tell a brief story. Had they been posed in identical directions, the feel would not be as interesting, but rather a "warehouse" inventory look to the display.

A few well-chosen pieces are the only decorative accents to strong form and simple color. Colors are closely related, keeping surprise to a minimum and comforting with serenity.

*Opposite* This chair is a thrift-store purchase painted black. The top arm-rail edge of the chair was finished with 2 parts copper metallic paint watered down with 1 part water and ¼ part liquid dish detergent. The mixture was painted on, then finger-tapped along the painted edge as if playing the piano to achieve an antique appearance. The paint was allowed to dry, then the edges of the chair were lightly distressed with sandpaper where natural wearing would have occurred over time.

The old cushion was re-covered with sturdy upholstery fabric stapled securely underneath the seat. To give the effect of an overstuffed back to the chair, a rectangular pillow was heavily fringed in a color and texture that mimic the carpet design, then arranged vertically at the back of the seat cushion. It appears to be part of the chair and offers inviting comfort.

The beauty of a simple arrangement of furniture and art is the peacefulness of the setting it creates.

Serenity and peacefulness are further carried out by the topic of the painting.

The tree captures our attention and the fence carries our eye to a distant place.

The dark table and chairs are bridged to the painting in a triangular shape, anchored by the compote filled with nature's bounty, and a hint of orange.

A palette of nature's woodland tones in browns, creams, tans, and muted greens grounds the room a rock-solid design as calm as the forest.

*Below* This buffet, purchased at a garage sale, had irreparable damage to its lower portions. These areas have been painted with flat-black paint to make them "disappear" as a problem and transform them into an integral part of the styling. Ornamental details were painted black to coordinate.

The family portrait of two generations in the original antique frame, from the same Victorian period as the buffet, makes imagining a story pertaining to those people a fine connection to the furniture. A simple black lamp illuminates yet yields importance to the buffet and portrait focal point.

*Above* This antique bureau, with small set-back drawers for jewelry or small personals and a diminutive ledge above the larger garment drawers, is typical of the Victorian style in furniture.

Styling it with a vintage photo of a Victorian wedding couple establishes the period of the vignette beautifully.

In keeping with that time are the other period accessories such as the old leather-bound books set at angles. Altering positions from leaf edge to spine adds interest to the arrangement.

## Buying Love-worn Furniture

The second time around can be wonderful. Second-hand furniture and decorative items are not only economical, they may be examples of style and craftsmanship unavailable from any other source.

There's a savvy art to selecting a used item worthy of bringing home at a reasonable price. Consider its sturdiness and "transformability" in terms of effort or expense.

Leather components should be in reasonable shape, requiring only restorative oiling. Wood can be renailed, stained, or painted. Metal can be refinished or painted. Fabric can probably be reupholstered, dyed, or patched with lace, trims, and ingenuity.

Styling should have appeal worthy of all the work you may have to invest in making the furniture or decorative item coordinate in your home. If it pleases and you can imagine it restored with style, risk buying!

*Left* This seating arrangement in a retro-period room is a study in recycling-style success.

The room itself is architecturally enhanced with a fireplace mantel created from what was once a pressed-tin wall shelf.

The pair of tufted-leather chairs with their hobnail details were originally used in an attorney's office. Their classic formality as a pair flanking the table is a high-style invitation to what the owners call their "coffee room."

The small table, now quite cozy with lamps and candles, is actually an old typewriter table. Its front wing arm can fold up to hold beverages, books, and small travel game boards appropriate for a quiet evening—just for two.

***Above Left*** Pillows layered for contrast are the perfect counterpoint for a classic image in a gilded frame. The pillows also work to support the purple and white theme of the room.

***Above Right*** Purple is a daring color for a room's walls. A painting of lilacs in bloom with accents of peachy gold, purple's complement, softens the color's intensity. Delicate patterns of red-bark branches create immediacy and interest, linking the nature theme with the lilacs and the bird on the tiny sculpted shelf.

***Left*** The white fan embroidery with cameos from the Holy Land is echoed in the patterned slipcover of the chair. Romantic touches abound to keep the room gentle.

*Below* This diminutive vignette shows how important size, shape, and proportion in a grouping of still-life items can be.

The styling here creates a delightful story idea. A figure of a young person resting beneath a tree— symbolized by the ivy—contemplates nature or perhaps knowledge.

The cord-wrapped tiles represent either incised tablets of old wisdom, or books handed down from other generations. Note the relationship of all within an invisible triangle.

*Above* The timeless effect of this charming arrangement is rather unusual, and that is part of why I like it. The paired lamps on either side of the centered warm-toned frame are quite large for such a small piece of furniture. The imposing vase is also large.

The print, the pair of shades, and the vase form a subtle and lovely visual diamond shape. This design is then supported by the symmetrical placement of the chairs on either side of the lamps. This arrangement is not only beautiful, but functional as well. People seated on the chairs can enjoy the soft light provided by the stylish lamps.

*Left* This simple bathroom has a decidedly classic feel and a warmth drawn from nature and fine craftsmanship.

Beginning with the wall treatment, a textured wallpaper was applied, then the wall was painted in warm earth tones.

The flat bathroom mirror was made elegant with a large old frame placed on top and attached with Velcro. Its beading detail is a pleasing textural contrast to the subtle wall pattern.

A simple relief sculpture of two classic figures lends a timeless feel enhanced with some seasonal branches from nature and a tea-stained lace doily.

Nothing jars the calm of this arrangement's styling details.

*Right* On another wall of the same bathroom, a charming as well as practical arrangement becomes a focal point.

The wooden shelf was purchased at a garage sale for $1.00. It was cut out underneath the shelf lip and the dowel was stained and added for a towel bar. Just off the master bedroom, the purple towel with its white tassel is a styling link.

The framed vintage print, found in a second-hand store, supports the detail of the shelf and the mirror frame opposite. The wooded landscape is the background for a symbolic story.

The statue of the child holds scented blossoms as though he stepped out of the trees with a sweet gift. The twigs echo the woods, the candle lights his way.

*Left* Clean and simple design is not uninteresting or ordinary. Texture and color, placement and style play roles as important or more so than in rooms with more design elements present than this one. Sunny warmth is apparent here, as in the rest of this home.

For a wall that has subtle tactual interest and can act as a neutral background to other style drama, take a cue from this room. The wall was texturized with joint compound applied with a putty knife in a random pattern. It was allowed to dry, then sponge-painted with crumpled plastic wrap. Two different shades of paint were used for a gentle blended effect.

The opaque Roman shades were chosen to complement the color of the windowsill. The candle was lit for this photograph, but would not ordinarily be so, for safety's sake. The candelabra effect of the bowl arrangement is artful and practical. Sponges, makeup items, guest soaps, and personal utilities are readily available for use.

The bird sculpture is an interesting accent choice, since the arrangement of branching bowls appears nestlike, perhaps in a symbolic tree. Whimsey is fun in decorating when only hinted at in such subtle touches.

*Above* From this perspective, it is easier to appreciate the symmetrical elegance of this simple arrangement in the window as well as its romantic theme and details.

The Victorian fringed scarf belonged to the owner's grandmother, so its significance in this private space was important. The graduated stack of embossed boxes topped with a vintage crystal perfume atomizer are suggesting a festive evening that might have occurred a generation or two ago.

Combining flowers with the decorative items is another romantic touch that was enhanced by nature—more than was originally intended. Fresh peonies were placed in the vase only half filled with water when the owner left on a trip. The peonies dried to this pale color with a faded quality of nostalgia that is quite charming and tinged with romance in this setting.

# Chapter 5

# Eclectic Vogue

*Some owners want to design their own over-the-top home-décor mode.*

Every age has its particular design fashion. However, when it comes to eclectic styling with elements from a variety of periods, creativity can be taken to the edge of extreme. Stopping just short of going over the edge is the delight I find in this sort of adventurous styling.

The drama of eclectic vogue styling comes from playing down some elements and emphasizing others in a way that cannot be missed, and certainly not ignored.

This home owner finds it impossible to part with favorite items when she finds something new. Whether it "goes" or not, she keeps the new and the old items and finds a way to integrate them with style.

Furniture and decorative items can sometimes border on the "edge" in design. That is where restraint in the styling comes in. The vogue "look" is high fashion, opu-

lent, exclusive, extravagant, one-of-a-kind, memorable, and totally marvelous. Little is held back to be ordinary.

Themes can be exploited for the dramatic, or just to hold dramatic items and styling together in a cohesive design that doesn't quite run all the way off the mark.

Sometimes the vogue value comes in designing a quite ordinary and comfortable room and adding just one powerful detail that has a surprise feature. That quality might be size, scale, color, texture, or subject matter.

There is a wistfulness in the historical styling atmosphere that this home owner captured. The rooms are meant to transport viewers to another time, social role, or to the appeal of a home designed for a person with a passion for the 18th or 19th century. Her intention was to have her home reflect the period she loves.

*Right* Embellishments of leafy branches, as seen on the cherubs, and scarf and ribbon accents—shades of Isadora Duncan, the infamous dancer who wore scarves everywhere—occur frequently throughout this owner's home.

Scarves are tied to or draped over various items such as urns, draperies, furniture, and shelving. For example, the embellishments on the clock are tied on with wire-edged ribbon.

A loop of ribbon secures the 100-year-old hand-carved crescent moon face to its high perch. Not in the sky, but certainly in a place of symbolic lofty importance in the room.

Purple and red are colors we attribute to the attire and castles of royal families. Why not treat one's self with such elegance?

*Eclectic vogue is when a little too much is just right.*

## Renaissance and Victorian complement each other here.

**Opposite** Michelangelo's classic painting of God creating Adam sets the tone of great works for the members of this household. A frame of size and importance and prominent placement makes a comfortable room even more extraordinary.

As architect and sculptor, as well as painter, Michelangelo would have approved of emphasizing the railing structure with white paint. Imagine it as dark wood and it disappears, creating a somber mood. The newel post was accented with a gold fleur-de-lis.

**Left** The secretary was purchased at a garage sale and finished with a cherry stain applied with a cloth. The dramatic beaded scarf is a vintage reproduction, but looks Victorian period to match the secretary. The gold-toned pot used for heating water is circa 1875. It and the graduated balls, rich with detail, are the contrasting elements in this opulent arrangement. Note the stacked, textured, red-lacquered boxes, the sprigs of ribbon-tied lavender, and the old books.

*Left Above* In this vogue-style home, pillows and framed family pictures are bountiful. A friendly hodgepodge of frame sizes, shapes, and colors lends spontaneity to this plush yet comfortable conversation area.

*Left Below* Made with vintage and new fabrics in many patterns and tactile textures, pillows were embellished with cording, tassel fringe, and beads to add sparkle and style. Colors both accent and complement the colors and tones of the pattern in the focal-point sofa. Though the sofa pattern is busy, the strong designs in the pillows hold their own and carry the eye around the room's window perimeter.

*Opposite* Seeing the sitting room area from above gives us the "planning point of view" quite clearly. Though there is a lot going on in this room's furniture and accessories, by angling the sofa and coffee-table cabinet from the corner to the room's center a sense of ease is achieved. The punch of hot magenta pink for the wing chair and a few pillows gives an edgy freshness balanced by conservative beige, cream, and white.

Hot magenta pink is complemented with a variety of greens, and muted walls, carpet, and draperies balance busy patterns.

Study the number, size, scale, and placement of the black carved items, offset by one white detailed statue.

*Right* The 1920s glasses and books belonged to the owner's grandfather. Gloves folded on the table are from the same estate sale as the cupboard doors above them.

*Opposite* The unique wall hanging is composed of the front carved-wood doors of an 1880s wine cabinet. Imagine them without the detail of the scrollwork above them or the beaded swag reflecting scrolled curves—not quite as outstanding a focal point.

*Below* Metal scrollwork above the cabinet doors was constructed from five separate metal pieces and hand-buffed with silver paint, using a cloth. The finish was worked on until it matched the intricate latches on the cabinet doors.

*Above* The three framed art and reliefwork pieces on this wall are quite visually tied together with not ribbons or scarves but beautifully hand-painted vining leaves and tendrils.

*Right* The leafy theme is carried out in three ways on this wall. Most prominent is the dried-leaf wreath that adds dramatic three-dimensional texture and rich natural color tones. Beneath it, the metal key-hook plaque has leaves in relief. Along the wainscoting, a row of subtle fleurs-de-lis have been hand-stamped

The rocker belonged to the owner's grandmother who received it for her 13th birthday. Old suitcases found at flea markets invoke a sense of travel to castles implied by this fireplace.

*Left* Styling for romance is easier when your collection of favorite items includes two- and three-dimensional theme objects.

The small art print in the style of Parrish and Fox is classic romantic myth in theme. The Cupid sculpture—with his tiny horn posed to take our eye to the print—is balanced in a triangle with the exotic ewer. The ewer has been draped with cord and placed atop a stack of old leather-bound books to meet the height of Cupid's horn. Its spout turns toward the print also.

In color palette, the yellow-green print mat complements the red-violet wall. The rusty earth colors in the urn, books, ewer, and sculpture rest upon the antiqued shelf. Its relief detail reflects the sculpted quality of the other items.

*Combine English and French eclectic elements.*

Riding to hounds on an English pillow and the wall's stamped French fleur-de-lis motif combine with a 1920s Union Pacific train station bench.

*Opposite* Nature's bounty appears not only heaped with dried roses and berries in baskets styled atop cupboards, but as hand-painted vine patterns on cupboard doors, wallpaper borders, and as hanging decorative embellishments.

*Below* The intricate details and strong forms of any of these drawer and door pulls transform the most ordinary cabinetry into vogue style. Some of these drawer pulls were purchased at an antique store and had their raised portions sanded lightly to expose a silvery chrome undercolor. Others have burnished brass effects and insets of gem colors, as though enameled or inset with semiprecious stones. Flatware pulls are an extraordinarily unexpected styling touch.

*In vogue style you can't have too many angels.*

**Left** The elaborate beribboned wreath takes up about the same amount of visual space as the cherub on the table, so a vertical balance is achieved. The angelic child's pose emphasizes the horizontal tabletop.

A fortunate find was this flea-market table in original condition. Gold fleur-de-lis designs were applied with a craft-store stamp.

**Opposite** The hand-painted wall is a fitting backdrop for this styled arrangement. Inexpensive, matching white resin wall plaques painted with sepia were mounted in a square formation. Another smaller plaque has been stained a deeper color and hung over the center meeting point of the larger ones.

An urn and an angel sculpture of the same color and surface treatment overlap the wall plaques, allowing the group of items to interact with one another as a whole.

The classic scene at the end of this home's hallway seems to have stepped from antiquity.

# Color

The palette of colors for this lovely bedroom could have been borrowed from a castle or a manor house, plus earth and foliage tones.

Gem tones from rich garnet purples to soft opal pink recall days of capes and gowns encrusted with sparkling stones.

This room avoids becoming trite or childlike by the way "days of yore" colors are suggested, not overpowering. Gentle not drastic contrast works well without bright white or heavy black.

# Style

The palatial ambience of this bedroom brings wishful fairy-tale elegance to life. The draped headboard effect is nothing short of royal in styling. Subtle textures in the fabric and its many folds express sumptuous luxury.

A sense of privacy and deepening space is made to happen by the way the draping comes around the sides of the bed. The frame hung within the drapery folds takes our eye inside and also acts as a visually stable headboard.

# Texture

The damask drapery effect, velvets, fringes, and soft bedding provide a wealth of textural experiences, both visually and to the touch.

Contrasting soft with crisp, fuzzy with smooth, delicate with rough, metallic with matte are ways to use texture to create heightened interest in a confined space.

Even the simple addition of the trim and stencil accents to the sculpted details of the cornice carries our eye upward.

# Accessories

Though this is an interior room, as with other rooms in this owner's home, there is always a grounding touch of nature to balance the romance and drama.

The three water birds atop the cornice and the green mat on the framed angel prints are hints of outdoors. The richness of the dark comforter is earthy and supports the wine colors of the array of pillows. The layering technique of placing light between dark was used.

*Right* The charming mirrored dresser reflecting the rest of the bedroom was a flea-market find refinished by stripping off old layers of paint. Cherry and walnut stains were mixed and applied to its wood surfaces. Cherry stain alone was used on the edging and trim, then a coat of satin polyurethane finish was applied.

The embellishment on the wall above the mirror was finished in the same manner as the dresser. It was hung on the wall to appear at first glance as if it is a part of the mirror frame itself.

The outdoors again merges with the interior of the bedroom through the vase of twigs and vines, the chubby sparrow, and the spikey grasses.

Mirror imagery doubles nature's impact with warm brown branches and green grasses. Twigs pick up the dresser's red/brown glow. A subtle touch is the twig that visually connects the two across the pot.

*Left* With a backdrop of putty walls and wallpaper-border wainscoting in a scrolled leaf pattern, outdoor elements—orchids, fish sculpture, floral pillows—are spirited here.

Classical furniture, urns, fabrics, and framed nymph print continue the retro theme.

A refurbished rocking chair, has a convenient lap throw draped over its ottoman. The owner's own baby shoes join candles, art, and books for personal spontaneity.

Candles in hanging as well as standing metal candleholders are mood setters and bring balance in their vertical alignment.

Fabrics and throws are draped throughout the room to invite warm, cozy, intimate conversation.

Old books, pillows, and sunlight dappling through a diffusing window shade remind us to slow down and restore ourselves.

# Acknowledgments

This book is dedicated to NYB who spoke life-changing words to me.

Thank you to my children who believe in me, my family who support me, my friends who encourage me, and my mother who loves me unconditionally. I love you all!

A special thank you to Jo Packham, Caroll Shreeve, Ray Cornia, and all the behind-the-scene staff at Chapelle for bringing this book to life and making this dream come true.

Thank you to my friends who allowed us, the crew, and you, the reader, into these wonderful extensions of themselves which they call home. Jeff and Tracey Merrill—farmhouse, Ken and Judy Hammerschmidt—cottage, Steve and Sharon Reynolds—nouveaux, Daniel and Cindy Beecher—vogue.

# Credits

PhotoDisc, Inc. Images (© 2000) 67

Jessie Walker 66

Marion Duckworth Smith 69r

# About the Author

*Connie Duran,* interior decorator and gift-shop entrepreneur, lives in a loft apartment above her main-floor business, Hen Feathers. As seen in Chapter 1, Duran's apartment is located in a commercial brick building constructed in 1888. The original interior brick walls have been incorporated into the decidedly chic design plan. Her shop, located on Ogden, Utah's Historic 25th Street, was featured in the book *Decorate Your Home for Christmas* by Jana Wilson.

Duran began her professional life as a store owner and designer after her four children David, Heather, Christopher, and Tyler were grown. Even though her family has grown with the addition of two grandchildren, Hanna and Hallie, Duran continues her design work by juggling several interior design projects and numerous indoor and outdoor wedding events.

# Index